Oooh! La! La!
Breakfasts

RECIPES BY
MAUGIE PASTOR

Owner of

Aaah! T'Frere's
Cajun Country Bed & Breakfast

*Jackie
C'est
Oooh! La! La!
Maugie*

Acknowledgements

It is with GRATITUDE

- *for God's love and guiding hand in our lives.*
- *for His gift of T'Frere's House to our family of six sons and two daughters and their spouses.*
- *for our wonderful staff – Carissa Borque, Alexis Billeaud, Mary Brown, and Missy Betts.*

Thank you for your loving care.

© MAUGIE PASTOR - 2002
ISBN # 0-9720007-0-4

Table of Contents

Tour of T'Frere's House 2
    House
    Entrance Hall
    Guest Porch
    Dining Room
    Mary Room
    Leah Room
    1890 Room
    Garden Room
    Garconniere
    Bourrée
    Fais Do Do
    Kitchen

Advanced Preparation 14
    Chez Mix
    Cooked Onions

Welcome Hors D'oeuvres 15
    Cajun Canapes - Crab Crustard
    T'Juleps

Breakfast Salads 16
    Mama's Apple Salad
    Orange Mint Melon
    Fruit Salad
    Warmed Grapefruit Baskets
    Old Fashion Pear Salad
    Strawberries, Bananas & Cream
    Cantaloupe, Grapes & Cottage Cheese
    Lemon Yogurt Fruit Salad

Oooh! La! La! Breakfasts Menus & Recipes

Oooh! La! La! Louisiane 25
    Cajun Angel Eggs
    Potato Farcie
    Acadiana Smoked Sausage
    Petite Crepes
    Pistolets

Oooh! La! La! Paris 31
Crisp Bacon slices
Cheese Cake Stuffed Pancakes
a trio of pancakes laced with homemade strawberry syrup, lemon syrup and Bananas Foster

Oooh! La! La! Mardi Gras 35
Eggs A La King
Royal Cheese Grits
Tomate Grille
Louisiana Yam in Pecan Syrup
Bread Pudding with Rum Sauce

Oooh! La! La! Mexico 41
Crawfish Enchiladas
Jalapeno Cheese Corn Bread
Refried Beans
Salade Mexico
Vanilla Flan

Oooh! La! La! Mama 45
Fig Preserves
Mama's Home Made Biscuits
Red Beans & Sausage

Oooh! La! La! Italy 47
Pizza Eggs
Bambino Potato
Vegetable Italia
Les Orrilles Du Couchon

Oooh! La! La! New Orleans 51
Po Boy Steak Sandwich
Po Boy Egg Sandwich
Marchand de Vin
Potato Au Gratin
Zydeco Green Beans
Pecan Pralines

Oooh! La! La! U.S.A. 55
Eggs Sunny Side Up
Hash Brown Potatoes
Hot Buttered Toast
Pain Per Du - French Toast

Lagniappe 57

Bon Jour Mon Amis,

My husband, Pat, and I were challenged when we bought T'Frere's House to become the "Best of the Best" in Acadiana. Working toward the same reputation we had earned after 35 years in the restaurant business, I smiled and said, "we can do that."

So grab a cup of coffee and sit down with me while we explore T'Frere's House and our eight world famous Oooh! La! La! Breakfasts. Colorful and picturesque, this book portrays the legendary accommodations and cuisine – a glimpse of what makes T'Frere's Bed & Breakfast the place to stay in Lafayette, Louisiana. Voted "Best of the Best" in Cajun country, T'Frere's House is a veritable cornucopia of our rich Cajun heritage – a real Louisiana treasure.

Designed with the host / hostess / chef in mind, you will discover the ease of preparing everything ahead (advanced prep), so that on the day of your party, food is "heat and serve ready" for oven, stove, or micro.

"Maugie"s Ideas" can be anything from advanced preparation seasonings, to how I cook bacon, or how to cook a round egg to fit on a pizza biscuit – all methods I have used in cooking over the years. From the Chez Mix to my Lagniappe French toast stuffed with cheese cake filling and topped with Bananas Foster, I share with you my breakfast recipes and ideas that make cooking for a breakfast / brunch party of 12 or more, easier, more fun, and less hassle – helpful hints that will let you enjoy your guests.

Life is full of wonderful challenges and creating this book was another one. It has been a true labor of love for Pat and I and our staff.

Enjoy!
Maugie Pastor

Aaah! T'Frere's House
Cajun Country Bed & Breakfast

CIRCA 1880

Landmark in Lafayette, Louisiana

Viola! Home of the world famous Oooh! La! La! Breakfasts. Acadian Colonial architecture inspired this engaging facade. Built of Louisiana red cypress hauled from the nearby Vermilion Bayou, the main house has six guest bedrooms. Nestled in the garden behind the big house is the Garconniere and two more guest rooms that offer the visitor seclusion and privacy.

Bienvenue A T'Frere's

The wide entrance hall speaks a warm "bienvenue" to the guests, inviting the visitor to stay a while. Discover the cajun mystique, that makes the innkeepers love of life, good food and serving God in the stranger who comes to their door, so contagious.

Guest Porch

Twilight time at T'Frere's House is enjoyed by guests on this beautiful enclosed glass porch overlooking the garden. T'Juleps and Crab Crustards served on the gallery begin the evening. While "la maison's" Cajun hosts regale the sojourner with endless possibilities to "laissez le bon temp rouler" (let the good times roll) in the Attakapas country their ancestors came to call home.

Maugie's Magic

Regal in presentation of both self and her creative Cajun cuisine, Marguerite "Maugie" Pastor is a former premiere restaurateur of Chez Pastor in Lafayette, Louisiana. She offers us a glimpse into what makes T' Frere's, her and husband Pat's bed and breakfast, the place to stay.

Dining Room

The Oooohs! and Aaaahs! emanating from the dining room have become the signature sounds of approval for Maugie's extraordinary feasts. Vivacious in her red silk pajamas, she artistically blends classic New Orleans cuisine and Cajun country soul food seasoned with an international flair. The Pastor's Oooh! La! La! Breakfasts have been voted "Best of the Best in Acadiana" for many years.

Photo compliments of Country Folk Art. Featured also on Better Homes & Gardens Food Network, Chef John Folse's "A Taste of Louisiana," PBS, ABC NEWS Country, Chili Pepper and Southern Living. Rated excellent Frommers & Fodor's Guide books.

The Mary Room

The 1800 queen size Mallard bed, signed by C. Lee, is a priceless Louisiana antique and the center piece of the Mary Room.

The Leah Room

The downstairs Leah Room is a retreat from the busy world. Comfy, cozy and quite inviting the dreamer to step back in time and enjoy your rest in this half canopy 1880 double bed.

The 1890 Room

The upstairs 1890 Room boasts two antique iron double beds and can sleep four. It's a great "giggly girls room" for friends and families.

The Garden Room

The upstairs Garden Room's dark green walls and antique white wicker furniture are complimented by a king size Twig bed. The privacy of an upstairs bedroom gives this room it's romantic appeal.

The Garconniere
(Boy's House in the back)

Nestled in "Les Jardin D'enarriere" (the gardens behind the house) is the Garconniere. Built for the young men of the house to entertain their friends, it was the perfect gathering place for an all night card game of BOURRÉE, or after an evening of dancing at the FAIS DO DO.

Today, the two rooms housed in the Garconniere are affectionately called The Bourrée and Fais Do Do rooms.

The Bourrée Room

A king size pencil post bed; walls of briquette entre poteau (brick between posts) and bousillage (clay moss white wash). Old fashion quilts and all the amenities that privacy demands are the inspiration for this boudoir.

The Fais Do Do Room

Hearts and flowers are the whimsical feeling of the queen size bed. Adorned with an old fashion hand knotted canopy, it beckons the bride to make her dreams come true.

T'Frere's Kitchen

The sensuous aromas coming from the kitchen, Mammy's smiling face over the fireplace, the old fashion Lavabo on the table, touches that are gentle reminders of days gone by. The legendary Cajun cuisine that is prepared in this kitchen and now presented in this book is a veritable cornucopia of the innkeeper's rich culinary heritage.

Enjoy,
Maugie

Advanced Preparation

Cooked Onions

6 sticks of margarine   1 teaspoon sugar
12 cups raw chopped onions

Saute till onions are wilted. Store in refrigerator till ready for use.

Maugie's idea! *2 cups raw onions & 1 stick of margarine = 1 cup cooked onion.*

Chez Mix

3 cups salt   1 cup cayenne pepper
1/4 cup black pepper

Place in covered container. Shake well. Ready for use in all the recipes in this book.

Maugie's idea! *This was the seasoning mix I used in all my recipes for our restaurant - Chez Pastor. I have discovered that 1 teaspoon of Chez Mix per pound of meat - fish - poultry is the perfect seasoning. Try it! You'll love it!*

Welcome Hors D'oeuvres & Cocktails

T'Juleps

2 quarts Crystal Light Ice Tea
1 cup Canadian Whiskey
2 oz. Peppermint Schnapps
Fresh Mint

Stir well and keep chilled in refrigerator. To serve, pour over ice and add a sprig of fresh mint.

Crab Crustards

10 narrow loaves of French bread, cut 1/2" thick. Yields approximately 22 to 24 slices per loaf. Set aside.

In large mixing bowl, add:
2 lbs. imitation crab meat   8 cups mayonnaise
2 8-oz. boxes Parmesan cheese   1/2 cup parsley flakes

Run imitation crab meat through meat grinder until coarsely ground. Add rest of ingredients. Mix well. Spread one heaping tablespoon per slice of French bread. Place in freezer containers, separating each layer with wax paper. Freeze.

Party time – Heat oven to 400 degrees. Heat frozen crab crustard 10 minutes and serve.

Mama's Apple Salad
yields 12 servings

3 large tablespoons mayonnaise
3/4 cup celery
3/4 cup grated cheese

6 apples
3/4 cup pecans

Place mayonnaise in mixing bowl. Cut apples into cubes, stirring into mayonnaise as you cut. This will keep apples from turning black. Cut celery into apples. Add cheese and pecans. Stir well.

Maugie's idea! *This is a portion control formula I worked out, if you need smaller amounts than 12.*

1 apple for every 2 people
1 heaping tablespoon of mayonnaise for every 2 apples
1/4 cup pecans for every 2 persons
1/4 cup grated cheese for every 2 apples
1/4 cup celery for every 2 apples

Orange Mint Melon

8 mint leaves
1/4 cup water
2 tablespoons Peppermint Schnapps
fresh mint

6 small oranges,
   peeled & seeded
4 tablespoons sugar

Puree in blender till minced finely. Pour in covered container and freeze. Serve frozen orange mint slush over cantaloupe or honey dew melon or both with a sprig of fresh mint.

Warmed Grapefruit Baskets

half grapefruit per guest   granulated brown sugar
Triple Sec liqueur   fresh kale garnish
                               orange

Slice grapefruit in half. Core grapefruit with coring knife. Place on baking sheet. Peel, seed, and quarter orange and place in center of grapefruit. Sprinkle each grapefruit with 1 teaspoon granulated brown sugar and 1/2 capful of Triple Sec liqueur. Place in 350 degree oven for 20 minutes. Line grapefruit dish with kale and place warm grapefruit on top.

Fruit Salad

yields 12 servings

2 cans chunky fruit salad
3 apples, cut up
3 oranges, cut up
3 bananas, sliced
1 cup pecans

12 strawberries
3 tablespoons sour cream
3 tablespoons juice from can
2 tablespoons sugar
1 cup mini marshmallows

Drain fruit salad. Save liquid. Add bananas, pecans, and marshmallows. In another bowl, mix sour cream, juice and sugar. Pour cream mixture into fruit. Mix well and chill. When ready to serve, top each serving with "fan cut" strawberries.

Old Fashion Pear Salad

yields 8 servings

1 head lettuce
1/2 cup grated cheese
8 kale leaves for garnish
8 tablespoons mayonnaise
1 29-oz. can pear halves
8 red cherries

Shred lettuce very thin. Place in ziplock with a little water and refrigerate. Chill one 29-oz. can of pears = 8 pear halves per can.

To assemble: Line small glass plates with kale. Top with shredded lettuce, 1 pear half, 1 teaspoon mayonnaise, grated cheese and cherry. Set on tray in refrigerator until ready to serve.

Strawberries, Bananas & Cream
yields 12 servings

2 8-oz. strawberry banana yogurt
4 tablespoons sour cream
4 cups sliced fresh strawberries
4 tablespoons condensed milk
4 tablespoons whipped cream
6 bananas, sliced

In a large bowl, mix yogurt, sour cream, condensed milk, and whipped cream until there are no lumps. Add fresh strawberries and chill. Bananas go well with this dish. Cut bananas into strawberries and cream right before serving.

Cantaloupe, Grapes & Cottage Cheese
yields 12 servings

cantaloupe   1 cup cottage cheese
1 cup of green or red grapes

Peel and dice cantaloupe, approximately 3 slices per guest. Break grapes away from stems, wash and drain. Mix grapes and cottage cheese together. Fill tall red wine glasses 1/2 full of cantaloupe and top with 1 tablespoon grape-cottage cheese mixture.

Lemon Yogurt Fruit Salad

yields 12 servings

2 8-oz. lemon yogurt
4 tablespoons condensed milk
4 tablespoons sour cream
4 tablespoons cool whip

2 cans chilled drained fruit cocktail
3 apples, cut up
3 oranges, peeled & seeded
4 bananas, sliced

In mixing bowl, add lemon yogurt, condensed milk, sour cream, and cool whip. Stir until cool whip is dissolved. Add drained fruit cocktail, apples, and oranges. Refrigerate. Add bananas just before serving. Stir well.

Oooh! La! La! Louisiane

Cajun Angel Eggs
eggs creme de la creme enhanced with a melange of cheese, broccoli, spinach and spices – C'est Oooh La La Sha!

Potato Farcie
potatoes, onions and cheese blended en casserole

Acadiana Smoked Sausage
hot and spicy grilled Cajun sausage

Petite Crepes
t'cakes topped with Louisiana cane syrup

Pistolets
hot French bread compliments this gourmet breakfast

Condiments
homemade fig preserves, cane syrup, maple syrup, butter

Maugie compliments this breakfast with Mama's Apple Salad.

Cajun Angel Eggs

yields 30 2/3 cup servings

Maugie's idea! *The beauty of this recipe is that it can be prepared ahead and frozen individually. I like to prepare an advance prep tray of the ingredients the day before I bake it. I prepare the cream cheese-egg mixture when I am ready to combine all the ingredients and bake the eggs - to freeze.*

Advanced Prep Tray

Cheeses
6 cups shredded Colby & Monterey Jack cheese
4 cups shredded American cheese
Place in large bowl. Cover with saran wrap.

Broccoli/Onion
2 lbs. frozen broccoli pieces
2 cups chopped onions
Place onion in deep pot and cover with water. Bring to a boil. Cook until onions are tender. Add frozen broccoli and bring to a boil. Cook three minutes longer. Drain through colander. Chop in blender until broccoli-onion mixture is a coarse puree. Set aside.

Spinach
1 10-oz. box chopped spinach
Microwave spinach in glass dish for 4 minutes on high. Remove, stir and return to microwave for 4 minutes more. Remove and squeeze all moisture from spinach. Cut with scissors into small pieces. Do not neglect this step. Set aside.

Cauliflower
1 1-lb. bag cauliflower
Place frozen cauliflower in glass plate. Microwave on high for 4 minutes. Remove, stir and return to microwave. Cook on high for 4 minutes more. Place cauliflower in blender and chop fine. Set aside.

Crackers & Jiffy Corn Bread Mix
1 8-oz. box Jiffy corn bread mix
12 crackers
Chop fine in blender. Set aside.

Parsley
1/2 bunch of parsley, yields about 3/4 cup chopped
Place fresh parsley in blender, stems torn off. Chop fine. Set aside.

Now your advanced prep is ready to combine with cream cheese-egg mixture.

Blender Prep

Cream Cheese-Egg Mixture
2 8-oz. packages cream cheese
Place in blender. Puree until soft.
Add to softened cheese in blender:
3/4 cup sour cream
3 teaspoons garlic puree
1 teaspoon cayenne pepper
2 teaspoons Chez Mix, page 14
Turn blender back on and mix well.

Eggs
To cream cheese mixture, add: 10 eggs
Mix well in blender with cream cheese. Pour into large mixing bowl. Your advanced prep is completed and you are ready to put it all together.

To Prepare & Cook Cajun Angel Eggs for Freezing

Preheat oven to 350 degrees.

Maugie's idea! I use small mold pans (see picture) to make individual orders. That way you can take from the freezer as many eggs as you need.

Spray mold pans well with no stick stray. I use my hands to spread it evenly so that the eggs don't stick. Set aside. Add to the cream cheese-egg mixture: shredded cheeses. Stir in broccoli-onion, cauliflower, spinach, corn bread-cracker mixture, and parsley. Stir well. Place 2/3 cup mixture into sprayed mold pans. Place mold pans, as many as will fit, into 2" deep baking pan. Cover with aluminum foil. Bake covered at 350 degrees. Bake until eggs rise in pan and pull away from sides. Approximately 35 to 45 minutes. Remove from oven and run a knife around edges of mold pan to keep eggs from sticking to sides. Place cooked eggs in mold pans in freezer. Allow to freeze overnight. The next day, run a sharp knife around the edge of eggs and pop them out. Wrap individually in aluminum foil and freeze, ready for party.

Day Before Party

Unwrap frozen eggs and place in glass pans, sides not touching. *Place glass pans in baking pan, cover with foil, refrigerate, ready for oven.

Maugie's Idea! *I do this because it keeps the eggs from turning brown on the top or the bottom.*

Party time - Preheat oven to 350 degrees. Place oven ready eggs and sausage in oven. Heat for 20 minutes.

Acadiana Smoked Sausage

Maugie's Idea! *I use Cajun smoked sausage as a breakfast sausage. Guests love it! If not available, try any of your region's good smoked sausage.*

Advanced Prep Sausage

1/2 link smoked sausage per serving

Slice sausage into about 1/2 inch thick slices, five slices per guest. Place on oven pan ready for oven. Refrigerate.

Party time - Place sausage and eggs in 350 degree oven for 20 minutes. When sausage is heated, blot with paper towel. Place on plate.

Potato Farcie

yields 12 servings

2 cups cooked onions, page 14	1 teaspoon sugar
1 stick margarine	10 slices American cheese
3 cups water	4 cups potato flakes
2 cups evaporated milk	3 tablespoons bacon bits
2 teaspoons Chez Mix, page 14	3 tablespoons sour cream

Place in heavy pot: water, milk, cooked onions, margarine, Chez Mix, sugar, and cheese. Heat until cheese melts. Turn fire off. Do not add potato flakes while mixture is boiling. Add potato flakes and stir well. Let stand for 5 minutes. Add 3 tablespoons bacon bits and 3 tablespoons sour cream. Mix well. Place 1/2 cup or 4 oz. scoop per person into glass casserole dishes, top with grated American cheese. Cover with saran wrap and refrigerate. Ready for microwave.

Party Time - Heat covered potatoes in microwave on defrost/warm cycle one minute for each potato.

Can be done ahead and kept warm.

Pistolets

Maugie's Idea! *I use "store bought" miniature French breads called pistolets (pistols). If unavailable, choose your favorite brown 'n serve rolls.*

1 pistolet per guest
Brush tops of bread with melted margarine or butter. Place on baking pans and cover with clean, wet dish cloth. Place in refrigerator. Party Time – Preheat oven to 350 degrees. Remove dish cloth. Heat in oven 10 minutes or according to package directions.

Maugie's Idea! *I cover them with a wet dish cloth because it keeps the bread moist in the refrigerator overnight. I uncover them just before going into the oven.*

Petite Crepes

Maugie's Idea! *I use frozen miniature pancakes.*

3 pancakes per serving
Spray baking pan. Place pancakes on pan in stacks of three. Brush tops with melted margarine or butter. Cover with paper towel. Spray paper towel with water. Place in refrigerator until time for heating. Just before heating, spray with water again. Lift paper towel after you spray, to be sure the paper isn't sticking. Heat them with paper towel still on pancakes. Place pancakes in the 350 degree oven when pistolets have five minutes left. That's all the time it takes to heat the pancakes.

Maugie's Idea! *I spray the pancakes in this manner because they too will come out moist and hot, as though I had just cooked them.*

Oooh! La! La! Paris

Crisp Bacon Slices

Cheese Cake Stuffed Pancakes

a trio of pancakes stuffed with cheese cake filling, laced with homemade strawberry syrup, lemon syrup, and Bananas Foster

Maugie's Idea! This is my favorite prepare ahead breakfast. Everything can be prepared ahead of time and frozen until the day of the party. Syrups keep nicely in the refrigerator. Try it. You'll love it!

Maugie compliments this breakfast with Orange Mint Melon.

Strawberry Syrup

yields 4 cups

In cooking pot away from stove add:
1 1/2 cups Smuckers strawberry jam
1 cup Smuckers strawberry syrup
1/2 cup Deep South strawberry syrup
1 cup sugar
1 stick of butter
1 egg

Stir ingredients thoroughly. Bring pot to stove. Turn fire on high, stirring until syrup begins to boil, then lower fire. Continue to stir. Takes about 10 to 15 minutes. **Never stop stirring. Syrup will curdle. Stir until sauce thickens.** Allow syrup to cool and pour into syrup pitcher. Keep refrigerated. Party time – Microwave on high till hot. Stir. Cool. Pour over oven heated pancakes.

Lemon Syrup

yields 4 cups

In cooking pot away from stove add:
2 lemons
2 beaten eggs
2 sticks of real butter
2 cups sugar

Zest lemons by peeling away the yellow skin only. Add zested lemon to cooking pot. Cut peeled lemon in half. Place strainer over cooking pot. Squeeze lemon into strainer over cooking pot. Add sugar, butter, and eggs to this mixture and stir thoroughly. Bring pot to stove and turn fire on high, stirring until syrup begins to boil, then lower fire. Takes about 10 to 15 minutes. **Never stop stirring. Syrup will curdle. Stir until syrup thickens.** Allow syrup to cool and pour into syrup pitcher. Keep refrigerated. Party time – Microwave on high till hot. Stir. Cool and pour over oven heated pancakes.

Bananas Foster Syrup

yields 4 cups

In cooking pot away from stove add:
2 sticks of butter (1 cup)
1 box dark brown sugar (2 cups packed)
1/2 teaspoon vanilla butter nut
1 cup light Karo syrup
1/2 teaspoon cinnamon
2 oz. banana liqueur
1/4 cup light rum
1 egg, well beaten

Mix all ingredients well in pot before bringing to fire. Bring pot to fire and turn on high, stirring until syrup begins to boil. Lower fire and stir until soft ball stage. Takes about 15 minutes. **Never stop stirring. Syrup will curdle.** Allow syrup to cool. Pour into syrup pitcher. Refrigerate. Party Time – Microwave on high until syrup is hot. Pour small amount in pot to heat bananas. Slice bananas into pot and heat. Spoon sliced bananas onto pancakes and pour rest of Bananas Foster from syrup pitcher.

Oven Cooked Bacon
Advanced Prep

Maugie's Idea! *This is a great way to cook large amounts of bacon for a party. You can cook it ahead and freeze. Bacon cooks nice and flat and this process also eliminates a lot of fat.*

Place cold bacon slices side by side on oven pan. Cover with same size pan. See picture below.

Bake in 500 degree oven using the following time schedule.
1. Bake 7 minutes. Remove covered pans from oven, keeping cover on. Pour grease from corner of pan into disposable container.
2. Return to 500 degree oven. Bake 5 minutes. Remove pan from oven. Repeat pouring grease from pan. Check bacon for doneness.
3. Return to 500 degree oven. Bake approximately 3 to 5 minutes. Repeat pouring grease from pan. Bacon should be flat and still soft, not quite done. Remove from pan and absorb the rest of the grease with paper towel. Place bacon layered in plastic container with wax paper between layers. Freeze. It's ready to go for your party.

Advanced Prep Tray

Place frozen bacon, 2 slices per guest, on baking pan (no cover) and place in refrigerator overnight. Party time - Cook bacon approximately 5 minutes more. Blot with paper towel. Voila! No messy grease clean up.

Cheese Cake Filling
Advanced Party Prep

2 8-oz. cream cheese
4 tablespoons sugar
4 tablespoons cool whip
4 tablespoons sour cream

Place all ingredients in blender and mix well. Place cheese cake filling in plastic container in refrigerator.

Cheese Cake Stuffed Pancakes
Advanced Party Prep

Hungry Jack frozen pancakes – 3 per guest – Cut frozen pancakes in half. Do not let them thaw before cutting. They will tear. Spread with cheese cake filling – not too thin, not too thick. Cover with other half like a sandwich.

Maugie's Idea! *Spray heavy duty baking pan with non stick spray. Place stuffed pancakes on pan. Spray with a light mist of water. Make an aluminum foil cover and spray with water. Cover pancakes tightly. This will keep your pancakes from burning and sticking and they will stay moist because of the light water spray. Place in refrigerator overnight, ready for party the next day.*

Party time – Heat syrups in microwave. Prepare syrups as directed. Set syrups aside in syrup pitchers ready to pour over pancakes.

Pancakes & Bacon

Preheat oven to 425 degrees. Place advance prep trays of covered pancakes and bacon in oven. Set timer for 5 minutes. When timer beeps, reset for another 5 minutes. Check bacon and if it is done, remove and blot with paper towel. Arrange criss crossed on plates. Bacon is usually done before pancakes and should be very crisp. If it is not done, leave in oven with pancakes. When timer beeps a second time (10 minutes), remove pancakes and arrange in a fan like fashion on plates, three per plate. Place bananas in syrup on one stack of pancakes. Pour Bananas Foster, lemon and strawberry syrups on stacked pancakes and serve immediately.

Oooh! La! La! Mardi Gras

Eggs A La King
eggs baked in white wine sauce au burre, courtesy over a ham-topped biscuit, and crowned with sauce a la Pastor

Royal Cheese Grits
grits, enhanced with cheese and garlic, a royalty dish

Tomate Grille
roasted tomato topped with parmesan cheese

Patate Douce
Cajun yams baked in a pecan syrup

Louisiana Bread Pudding with Rum Sauce
classic Cajun country dessert

Maugie compliments this breakfast with Warmed Grapefruit Baskets.

Eggs A La King

biscuits (super size canned) eggs
ham Pastor sauce

Biscuits

1 biscuit per guest

Preheat oven to 350 degrees. Using your fingers, press out raw biscuit to the size of a cooked egg. Place biscuits on baking tray and bake at 350 for 10 minutes. Cover with wet cloth and refrigerate. Party time - Finish cooking at 450° for 6 minutes along with eggs, tomatoes, and yams.

Maugie's Idea! *I use the muffin top pan to bake the eggs in the oven. See picture. They come out perfectly round and set nicely on top of the ham and biscuit.*

Egg Tray

1 egg per guest

Butter muffin top pans with lots of butter. Add a teaspoon of white wine to each round indention in buttered pan. Break open egg into butter/wine mixture. Refrigerate. Party time -

Bake eggs in 450° oven for 6 minutes, until yellow of eggs turn white.

Ham

1 slice of ham per guest

Party time - Place ham on top of cooked biscuit, topped with cooked egg. Finish Eggs a la King with Pastor sauce.

Tomate Grille
1 tomato yields 3 servings

1 sliced tomato per guest

Turn tomato upside down. Cut one very thin slice from bottom. Cut second slice about 1/2" thick; middle slice about 1/2" thick; third slice - turn tomato right side up and cut crown away. Place on baking sheet. Lightly sprinkle with parmesan cheese and parsley flakes. Place in refrigerator until party time. Party time – Bake with eggs, yams, and biscuits at 450 degrees for 6 minutes.

Louisiana Yams

1 frozen yam patty per guest

Advanced prep – Place frozen yam patties in glass pan. Top with Bananas Foster syrup, page 32, and pecans. Place in refrigerator until party time. Party time – Place with eggs, tomatoes, and biscuits at 450 degrees for 6 minutes.

Party Time – Preheat oven to 450 degrees. Place eggs and uncover cold partially cooked biscuits, tomato and yams in oven for approximately 6 minutes, or until yellow of egg turns white. Place cooked egg on warmed biscuit that has been topped with a slice of ham. Cover with warmed Pastor sauce.

Pastor Sauce
yields 8 cups

2 cups cooked onions, page 14
1 stick margarine
2 teaspoons Chez Mix, page 14
1 teaspoon sugar

1 teaspoon instant chicken
    bouillon granules
1 cup flour
8 cups evaporated milk

Saute onions, margarine with Chez Mix, sugar, chicken bouillon granules till onions are well blended. Add 1 cup of flour to make a white roux and stir till oil is absorbed. Turn fire down and add evaporated milk, stirring mixture with a whisk to get the lumps out. When all lumps are out, switch to a spatula to stir the mixture. While constantly stirring the sauce, be sure to scrape the bottom and sides of the pot to prevent the sauce from turning brown. Keep stirring until sauce thickens – about 15 minutes. Set aside or chill till party time.

Royal Cheese Grits
yields 12 servings

In heavy stove pot:
6 cups water
2-1/3 cups old fashion grits
1-1/2 teaspoon salt
3/4 teaspoon cayenne pepper
1 teaspoon garlic powder

1/4 lb. margarine
7 slices American cheese
4 oz. cream cheese
1 teaspoon sugar

Allow water to come to full boil. Add seasoning. Slowly stir in grits. Turn fire down to simmer and cover. Check in 3 minutes. Cook covered for about 20 minutes, checking every few minutes and stirring to keep grits from becoming lumpy. When grits are done, add cheeses and margarine. Stir until dissolved. Cover and leave on simmer, ready to dish up for party.

Maugie's Idea! *This is a formula I worked out for adding 2 more servings or however many you need: 2 servings = 1 cup water + 5 tablespoons grits + 1/2 teaspoon salt + 1/4 teaspoon garlic powder + 1/4 teaspoon cayenne pepper.*

Louisiana Bread Pudding with Rum Sauce
yields 12 servings

6 cups evaporated milk
2 cups sweet milk
2 cups sugar
8 egg yolks, keep whites

2 sticks melted butter
3 teaspoons vanilla
8 hamburger buns,
  cut into pieces

Soak hamburger buns in milk. Add melted butter. Let set for 30 minutes. Cream egg yolks and sugar. Add vanilla and blend well. Pour into 9" x 13" glass baking dish and bake in preheated oven at 350 degrees for 30 minutes. Lower heat to 300 degrees and cook another 30 minutes. Top with meringue. Just before serving, top with rum sauce.

Meringue

8 egg whites   3 tablespoons sugar

Pour egg whites into a bowl. Place bowl over a pan of warm water. Mix with electric mixer slowly adding sugar until firm.

Rum Sauce
yields 2 pints

2 cups evaporated milk
4 tablespoons cornstarch
1/3 cup sugar
1/3 cup rum

1 teaspoon vanilla
2 tablespoons butter
1/2 cup cherry juice

Dissolve cornstarch in milk and blend in sugar. Add vanilla and melted butter. Bring to a boil, stirring constantly until thickened. Remove from heat and add cherry juice and rum. Blend well. Serve over bread pudding that has been heated and topped with meringue.

Royal Cheese Grits, Tomate Grille, and Patate Douce. Viola! Oooh! La! La! Mardi Gras.

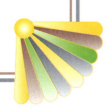

Oooh! La! La! Mexico

Crawfish Enchiladas
cheesy sauced crawfish etouffee wrapped in flour crepes

Jalapeno Cornbread
moist and loaded with onions, cheeses, jalapeno

Refried Beans
refried beans with a Cajun twist

Salade Mexico
roma tomato, cucumber, parsley, green onions in Italian dressing

Vanilla Flan
traditional - delicious - uniquely Louisiana

Maugie compliments this breakfast with Fruit Salad.

Crawfish Enchiladas
yields 35 - 5" enchiladas

Crawfish Etouffee

3/4 cup oil
8 cups chopped onion
1 cup chopped celery
3 teaspoons minced garlic
1/4 cup Italian tomato paste

3 teaspoons Chez Mix, page 14
3 lbs. crawfish
1/4 cup flour
1-1/2 cups water
1 stick of butter

Season crawfish with Chez Mix and set aside.

Maugie's Idea! In blender, place 1/4 lb. butter and 1 cup crawfish. Puree and set aside. This adds flavor.

Pour oil into heavy pot and heat on medium. Add onions, celery, minced garlic, tomato and pureed crawfish. Cover vegetable mixture. Etouffee means to smother. Cook until vegetables are well done. Stir in crawfish tails and simmer for 10 minutes – no longer. Crawfish will over cook. Stir often. Dissolve flour in water and add to pot. Bring back to a boil and cook for 15 minutes, stirring often. Set aside.

Rotel Cheese

1/2 cup cooking oil
4 cups chopped onions
1 teaspoon minced garlic
2 lbs. Velveeta cheese, cut

1 teaspoon salt
1 teaspoon sugar
2 10-oz cans Rotel tomato

Saute onions and garlic in oil. Add Rotel tomatoes, salt, and sugar. Cook until mixture begins to stick, stirring often. Add cheese. Cook until cheese is melted, stirring constantly. Set aside. Spread about 2 tablespoons of crawfish etouffee and 2 tablespoons of Rotel cheese on five inch flour tortillas and roll into Enchilada.

Maugie's Idea! I freeze these in stacks, between layers of wax paper. Take them out the night before. Place single layer in glass baking pans. Spray aluminum foil with water. Cover enchiladas tightly with "water sprayed foil" and place foil covered pans on baking sheet. Heat in oven at 350 degrees for 20 minutes. Viola! they will be hot and moist. No dried shells. The baking pan and the sprayed aluminum foil keep them from drying out. Top them with Rotel cheese just before serving.

Jalapeno Cheese Corn Bread

yields 12 - 2" square servings

3 boxes Jiffy corn bread
3 eggs
1 cup milk
1/2 cup Jalapeno peppers, chopped
2 cups Sargento Mexican 4 cheese

4 cups cooked onion
1/4 lb. margarine
2 cups red/green bell pepper
2 cups Monterey Jack cheese

Mix all ingredients together. Pour into greased 9" x 13" glass pan. Bake at 350 degrees for 45 minutes.

Refried Beans

yields 12 servings

1/2 stick margarine
2 cups chopped onions
1 teaspoon garlic powder

2 teaspoons Chez Mix
4 tablespoons sour cream
4 cans Old El Paso
    Traditional refried beans

Saute onions in margarine until onions are clear. Add beans, garlic powder, Chez Mix. Cook about 10 minutes. Stir in sour cream.

Salade Mexico

yields 12 servings

10 Roma tomatoes
2 cucumbers
Lawry's seasoned salt

1 cup green onions chopped
1/4 cup fresh chopped parsley
Good Seasons Zesty Italian

Slice tomato and cucumber. Add parsley and green onions and season with Lawry's seasoned salt and Good Seasons Zesty Italian.

Vanilla Flan

yields 12 cups

4 cups sugar
1 cup flour
4 cups milk

2 sticks butter
1 teaspoon vanilla butter nut
3 cups evaporated milk

Put all ingredients in sauce pan and stir thoroughly. Cook over low heat, stirring constantly until sauce thickens. Leave it plain vanilla, or add coconut, lemon, or chocolate.

Oooh! La! La! Mama

Mama's Homemade Biscuits

Homemade Fig Preserves

Red Beans & Sausage

A serving of red beans and flaky biscuits fill you up with warmth, just like a hug from Mama. Homemade fig preserves are the perfect "icing of the cake."

Maugie compliments this breakfast with
Strawberries, Bananas & Cream.

Red Beans & Sausage

2 lbs. dried red beans
2 cups sliced smoked sausage
1 large ham bone (the part that's left when you can't slice anymore)
1/2 cup honey
water

5 cups chopped onions
1 teaspoon cayenne pepper
2 tablespoons garlic puree
1 cup chopped celery
2 capfuls liquid smoke

Soak red beans overnight in enough water to cover them. Rinse and drain. In large pot, add beans and the rest of the ingredients. Cover with water that is about two inches above ingredients. Bring to a boil. Stir well and turn fire down. Simmer for about four hours. Beans should be "mushy" when done.

Mama's Homemade Biscuits

yields 30 biscuits

Preheat oven to 375 degrees.
1 40-oz. box Pioneer buttermilk biscuit mix
1 cup Crisco butter flavor all vegetable shortening
Knead the above with kneading knife.
2-1/2 cups sweet milk   juice of 1/2 large lemon
1 teaspoon sugar in milk

Pour milk mixture into kneaded flour and stir with fork until milk mixture is absorbed. Sprinkle dough liberally with flour. Wet cabinet top thoroughly with water. Overlap wax paper onto wet cabinet top, being sure wax paper adheres to cabinet. Sprinkle liberally with flour. Place dough ball onto floured paper and knead four times. Do not over knead. Dough will be tough. Roll out 1/2" thick with rolling pin. Cut with 3" biscuit cutter and place in glass pans, sides not touching. Bake at 375 degrees 15 to 20 minutes.

Fig Preserves

5 lbs. sugar   10 lbs. fresh figs
1-1/2 cups water

Place figs in large heavy pot. Pour sugar and water over figs. Cook over low fire until syrup has turned from lavender color to brown. Figs should be done in 1-1/2 to 2 hours. Follow canning procedure to preserve figs.

Oooh! La! La! Italy

Pizza Eggs
pizza butter biscuit, tomato basil sauce, pizza egg, Pastor sauce, cooked onions, green & red bell pepper, bacon bits and mozzarella and cheddar cheeses

Vegetable Italia
Italian vegetable blend seasoned and roasted

Bambino Potatoes
steamy parsley buttered newborn potatoes

Les Orrilles du Couchon
Cajun pigs' ears – a delightful pastry laced with cane syrup and pecans

Maugie compliments this breakfast with Old Fashion Pear Salad.

Advanced Prep Pizza Eggs

Pizza Biscuits

12 Grand "supersize" canned biscuits

Preheat oven to 400 degrees. Spread flour on wax paper. Place canned biscuits on floured wax paper. With your finger tips, pick up biscuit and flatten out to the size of a cooked egg. Place on metal pans. Bake at 400 degrees for 13 minutes. Remove from oven. Turn oven down to 325 degrees for pizza eggs. Allow to cool. Cover with wet dish cloth and refrigerate. Ready for party time.

Pizza Eggs

1 cup chopped onion
4 tablespoons margarine
10 eggs

1 teaspoon Chez Mix, p. 14
1/4 cup evaporated milk
1/2 cup grated American cheese

Maugie's Idea! To cook the eggs into a round shape the size of a small pizza, I use what are called Muffin Top pans. See picture. They are aluminum and about 10" x 14" and have six round indents about 1/2" deep. I love these pans and a little imagination.

Preheat oven to 350 degrees. Grease muffin pans and set aside. Saute onions in margarine until clear. Set aside 1/2 cup of cooked onions for pizza topping. Into mixing bowl, break open eggs. Add Chez Mix, evaporated milk, and grated cheese. Slowly add cooked onion-margarine mixture, beating egg mixture as you do. This is called "tempering" and if done right, the hot onion mixture will not cook the egg. Pour mixture into greased skillet and cook until soft curl stage. Spoon undercooked egg (still enough liquid to cook into a round shape) into greased muffin top egg pan. Cook at 325 degrees for about 10 minutes or until eggs are cooked. Refrigerate until party time.

Tray Assembly for Pizza Topping

12 cooked biscuits
1 cup bacon crumbles
2 cups Mozzarella cheese
1/2 cup black olives, sliced
1/2 cup green/red bell pepper

12 pizza eggs
1 cup Ragu basil tomato sauce
1 cup Pastor sauce, page 38
1/2 cup cooked onion

Party Time – assemble as you would a pizza

1. Biscuit
2. Ragu basil tomato sauce
3. pizza egg
4. Pastor sauce
5. sauteed onion

6. bacon crumbles
7. Mozzarella cheese
8. black olives
9. green & red bell pepper

Heat pizza egg in 350 degree oven until cheese melts. About 10 minutes. Serve immediately.

Vegetable Italia

1 - 2 lb. package frozen Italian vegetables
2 teaspoons Lawry's seasoned salt
1 teaspoon garlic powder
1 tablespoon olive oil

Pour vegetables into microwaveable dish. Add seasonings. Place back in freezer until party time. Party time – Stir well. Microwave on high 4 minutes and stir. Repeat process until vegetables are steamy.

Bambino Potatoes

2 lbs. Irish potatoes
2 teaspoons Chez Mix, page 14
1 cup fresh minced parsley
1 stick of butter

Cut potatoes into 1" cubes leaving skin on. Boil until tender. Season with Chez Mix, butter and fresh chopped parsley. Refrigerate until party time. Party time – Cover with foil and heat at 350 degrees for 20 minutes.

Les Orrilles du Couchon

Maugie's Idea! *In Italy, Les Orrilles are called Cenci alla Fiorentina (deep fried sweet pastry). Cajuns love their pigs' ears with a salty dough, slathered in cane syrup and pecans.*

1 cup all purpose flour	1/4 teaspoon salt
1/3 cup water	

Gradually add water to flour and salt, using your finger tips to absorb all the water. Using a little flour, knead and divide into 1" balls. Roll out dough into ovals that are paper thin. Place in layers of wax paper, ready for frying. Fry in deep fat 350 degrees, using handle of long wooden spoon. Sink the dough down and hold a few seconds. These resemble pigs' ears. Coat with Orrilles syrup and pecans.

Les Orrilles du Couchon Syrup

1 cup cane syrup	1/4 cup sugar
1/4 pinch salt	1/2 cup toasted pecans
1 teaspoon butter	

Boil syrup, sugar, and salt over medium heat, stirring constantly. Cook until hard ball stage. Coat orrilles with syrup and pecans.
Store in air tight container.

Oooh! La! La! New Orleans

Po Boy Egg Sandwich
eggs, butter, cream and Cajun seasonings smothered and sandwiched on a po-boy bun

Steak Po Boy Sandwich
hamburger steaks topped with Marchand de Vin

Zydeco Green Beans
green beans (l'haricot) hot and spicy

Potatoes au Gratin
sliced baked potatoes in a creamy cheese sauce

Pecan Pralines

Maugie compliments this breakfast with Old Fashion Pear Salad.

Po Boy Eggs
yields 12 servings

12 pistolets, miniature po boy, tops buttered
1 teaspoon sugar
1/2 cup grated American cheese
1/4 cup evaporated milk
1 cup Pastor sauce, page 38
11 eggs
1/2 teaspoon fresh basil
1 stick margarine
1 cup chopped onions
3/4 cup green & red bell pepper
1/4 teaspoon garlic powder
1 teaspoon Chez Mix, page 14

Saute onions and bell pepper in margarine till wilted. Set aside. In mixing bowl, break open eggs. Add garlic powder, Chez Mix, basil, sugar, cheese and cream. Beat well. Pour egg mixture into skillet of sauteed onions and bell pepper, stirring well. Scramble eggs on high fire until soft curl stage. Eggs are beginning to cook, but not all the way. Add Pastor sauce to partially cooked eggs and finish cooking. Eggs will be soft and creamy, but they are cooked. Spoon this mixture onto 12 pistolets. Set on baking tray for party time. Cover with wet cloth. This keeps the bread from drying out. Party time – Bake at 450 degrees for 5 to 8 minutes, until golden brown. Serve immediately.

Hamburger Steak Po Boy
yields 12 - 4-oz. hamburger steaks

3 lbs. ground chuck
3 regular hamburger buns
cooking oil
3 teaspoons Chez Mix, page 14
3 eggs

Run hamburger buns through food chopper. Do not substitute. Mix ground chuck, Chez Mix, and eggs until bread cannot be seen. Important! Using cooking oil on your hands, form miniature hamburger patties to fit pistolets. Cook patties in heavy pot with a little oil until done. Place cooked hamburger patties on buttered pistolets on baking tray. Cover with wet cloth. Set aside. Party time - Bake at 450 degrees for 5 to 8 minutes until golden brown. Serve immediately.

Marchand de Vin Sauce

1 stick margarine
1 cup chopped onion
1 cup sliced fresh mushrooms
1/2 cup green & red bell pepper
1 teaspoon Chez Mix, page 14
1 tablespoon brown sugar
4 tablespoons brown flour
1/2 cup red wine
2 teaspoons chicken base
2 cups water

Saute onions until wilted. Add peppers, mushrooms and seasonings. Saute 5 minutes. Stir in brown flour. Add chicken base, water and red wine. Simmer 15 minutes. Set aside. Party time – Heat and spoon over oven-heated po boys just before serving.

Zydeco Green Beans
yields 12 servings

4 tablespoons vegetable oil
2 cups chopped onion
1 teaspoons garlic puree
1/2 teaspoon cayenne pepper
3/4 cup milk

4 14.5oz. cans green beans, rinsed
1 can cream of mushroom soup, 10-3/4 oz.
1 cup French fried onions

Drain and rinse beans and set aside. Saute onions in oil until clear. Mix all ingredients together and place in baking dish. Bake at 350 degrees for 30 minutes. Party time – Reheat and serve.

Potatoes au Gratin
yields 12 servings

Maugie's Idea! *I cheat on this one. I "put the Cajun" to Betty Crocker's Sour Cream & Chives. I also short cut the cooking process by boiling the potatoes before I add the sauce to them.*

2 5-oz. boxes Betty Crocker Sour Cream & Chives
   100% Real Potatoes

Remove potatoes from box. Place in pot of boiling water, enough water to cover. Boil until tender. Drain and place in 9" x 12" baking dish.
In separate cooking pot add:

1 stick margarine
2 cups chopped onion
1 cup red & green bell pepper
1 teaspoon garlic puree
1/2 teaspoon cayenne pepper
1/2 cup potato flakes, to thicken

2 cups water
1 cup Pastor sauce, page 38
1-1/2 cups cheddar cheese
2 bags Betty Crocker
   sauce mix

Saute onions in margarine until clear. Add all the rest of the ingredients, stirring until sauce is well blended. Pour sauce over potato mixture. cook in 350 degree oven 45 minutes. Party time – Cover with foil. Reheat at 350 degrees for 30 minutes.

Pecan Pralines
yields 24

2 cups sugar
1/2 cup white Karo syrup
1/2 cup water

2 cups pecan halves
1/2 stick margarine
1 tablespoon vanilla butter nut

In heavy pot, combine sugar, syrup, water and pecans. Over medium heat, stirring often, cook until sugar is dissolved. Cook, stirring occasionally, until mixture reaches soft ball stage (small amount forms a soft ball when dropped in water). Remove pot from heat, add margarine and vanilla. Allow candy to cool. Whip until mixture changes to a lighter color and becomes creamy. Drop by tablespoons on buttered pan.

Oooh! La! La! U. S. A.

U.S.A. Eggs Sunny Side Up
good ole eggs cooked U.S.A. way

Bacon Crisp
bacon crisped in the oven

Hash Brown Potatoes
potatoes and onions are ettouffed Cajun style

Hot Buttered Texas Toast
thick sliced bread lavished with butter

Pain Per Du
"lost bread" – delicious "Cajunized" French toast

Maugie compliments this breakfast with
Lemon Yogurt Fruit Salad.

Eggs Sunny Side Up

Cook eggs U.S.A. style - Sunny Side Up!

Into skillet place enough oil to roll around the bottom. To get the full flavor of the egg, never get the oil too hot. Break open eggs into hot oil. Use a spatula to spoon hot oil over eggs. When yellow of egg turns white, egg is cooked. Remove from skillet and serve.

Maugie's Idea! *When cooking eggs for a crowd, they can be fried ahead and set aside. To reheat eggs, I fill a skillet with water, bring it to a boil, then turn down to simmer. Place egg on a spatula, run through simmering water, keeping egg on spatula. Viola! Egg is hot in seconds.*

Bacon Crisp

See page 33.

Hash Brown Potatoes

6 white potatoes
2 cups chopped onions
3 tablespoons Chez Mix
1/2 cup cooking oil

Peel and slice potatoes. Boil potatoes and onions in enough water to cover. This shortens cooking time. When potatoes are beginning to soften, drain onions and potatoes well. Heat oil in heavy skillet. Season potatoes and onions. Fry potatoes and onions until brown, turning often.

Hot Buttered Texas Toast

thick sliced white bread   melted butter

Brush thick sliced bread with butter. Toast in oven until brown.

Pain Per Du - French Toast

yields 45 slices

2 loaves narrow French bread
9 eggs
1-1/2 cups sugar
1 teaspoon vanilla butter nut

1 stick butter
1 cup evaporated milk
3/4 cup sweet milk
1/2 cup cooking oil

Cut French bread into 1" slices and set aside. Mix eggs, sugar and vanilla butter nut. In microwave, melt butter and warm milk. Mix together. Slowly pour milk-butter mixture into eggs, beating all the while. This is called "tempering" the eggs so that the warmed mixture doesn't cook the eggs.

Maugie's Idea! *I do this so that the butter will be evenly distributed into the bread when bread is soaked.*

Pour egg-milk mixture into deep dish. Soak bread slices in mixture, turning to be sure bread is thoroughly soaked. Place soaked bread in flat dish ready to cook. Pour enough oil in electric skillet to cover bottom generously. Heat to 325 degrees. Cook soaked bread, turning as bread browns, abut five minutes total.

Maugie's Idea! *My kids loved this with powdered sugar or cane syrup. I also have stuffed them with Cheese Cake Filling, page 34, and topped with Bananas Foster Syrup and bananas, page 32. It's soo goood, Sha!*

Lagniappe!
French Toast Stuffed with Cheese Cake Filling & Topped with Bananas Foster

INDEX

1890 Room 8	Mama's Apple Salad 16
Acadiana Smoked Sausage 29	Mama's Homemade Biscuits 46
Bacon Advanced Prep Tray 33	Marchand de Vin 52
Bacon Oven Cooked Advanced Prep 33	Mary Room 6
Bacon Party Time 33	Meringue 39
Bambino Potatoes 49	Old Fashion Pear Salad 20
Bananas Foster Syrup .32	Oooh! La! La! Italy Menu 47
Bouree Room 11	Oooh! La! La! Mama Menu 45
Bread Pudding 39	Oooh! La! La! Mardi Gras Menu 35
Cajun Angel Eggs .26-28	Oooh! La! La! Mexico Menu 41
Cajun Canapes - Crab Crustard 15	Oooh! La! La! Louisiane Menu 25
Cantaloupe, Grapes & Cottage Cheese 22	Oooh! La! La! New Orleans Menu 51
Cheese Cake Filling Advanced Party Prep 34	Oooh! La! La! Paris Menu 31
Cheese Cake Stuffed Pancakes 34	Oooh! La! La! U.S.A. Menu 55
Chez Mix 14	Orange Mint Melon .17
Cooked Onions 14	Pain Per Du 57
Crawfish Enchiladas .42	Pancakes Party Time .34
Dining Room 5	Pastor Sauce 38
Eggs A La King 36	Pecan Pralines 54
Eggs Sunny Side Up .56	Petite Crepes (Pancakes) 30
Entrance Hall 3	Pistolets (French bread) 29
Fais Do Do Room 12	Pizza Biscuits 48
Fig Preserves 46	Pizza Eggs 48
Fruit Salad 19	Po Boy Eggs . . . . ,52
Garconniere 10	Potato Farcie 28
Garden Room 9	Potatoes Au Gratin 53
Grits Royal Cheese 38	Red Beans & Sausage 46
Guest Porch 4	Refried Beans 43
Hamburger Steak Po Boy 52	Rotel Cheese 42
Hash Brown Potatoes .56	Rum Sauce 39
Hot Buttered Toast 56	Salade Mexico 44
House 2	Strawberries, Bananas & Cream 21
Jalapeno Cheese Corn Bread 43	Strawberry Syrup Advanced Party Prep 32
Kitchen 13	Syrup Party Time 34
Leah Room 7	T'Juleps 15
Lemon Syrup Advanced Party Prep 32	Tomate Grille (Grilled Tomato) 37
Lemon Yogurt Fruit Salad 23	Vanilla Flan 44
Les Orrilles Du Couchon 50	Vegetable Italia 49
Les Orrilles Du Couchon Syrup 50	Warmed Grapefruit Baskets 18
Mama's Apple Salad .16	Yam Louisiana (Sweet Potato) 37
Mama's Homemade Biscuits 46	Zydeco Green Beans .53

ORDERING INFORMATION

Aaah! T'Frere's Oooh! La! La! Breakfasts

3 WAYS TO ORDER:

Mail check with order form to: Aaah! T'Frere's Oooh! La! La! Breakfasts
1905 Verot School Road
Lafayette, Louisiana 70508

Call in your credit card order: 1-800-984-9347

Fax your credit card order: 1-800-984-9347

Please feel free to copy this form and pass it on to a friend.

Oooh! La! La! Breakfasts

Maugie Pastor
c/o Aaah! T'Frere's House • 1905 Verot School Road
Lafayette, Louisiana 70508

Please send me _____ copies @ $12.50 each . . . . ._____

8% sales tax . . . . ._____

Plus postage and handling @ 2.50 per book . . . . ._____

Total . . . ._____

Enclosed is my: ❏ Check   ❏ Money Order

❏ Visa   ❏ MC   ❏ American Express   ❏ Discover

Credit Card Account Number_____Exp. Date_____

Signature_____

Make check/money order payable to T'Frere's House. Sorry, no C.O.D.'s, foreign checks or currency accepted.

Shipping address: (Please Print)

Name _____

Address _____

City _____

State_____Zip_____